The Young Geographer Investigates
Mountains

Terry Jennings

Oxford University Press

Oxford University Press, Walton Street, Oxford OX2 6DP

Oxford   New York   Toronto
Delhi   Bombay   Calcutta   Madras   Karachi
Petaling Jaya   Singapore   Hong Kong   Tokyo
Nairobi   Dar es Salaam   Cape Town
Melbourne   Auckland

and associated companies in
Berlin   Ibadan

Oxford is a trade mark of Oxford University Press

ISBN 0 19 917072 X (Paperback)
First published 1986
Reprinted 1988, 1990, 1991
ISBN 0 19 917078 9 (Hardback)
First published 1986
Reprinted 1990, 1991

© Terry Jennings 1986

Typeset in Great Britain by
Tradespools Limited, Frome, Somerset
Printed in Hong Kong

Acknowledgements

The publishers would like to thank the following for permission to reproduce transparencies:

Aspect Picture Library: p. 4 (top and bottom left), p.13 (bottom), p. 35 (right),
p. 37 (bottom); Australian Information Service, London: p. 33 (2nd from bottom
and bottom right); Biophoto Associates/David Mardon: p. 26; British
Geological Survey: p. 7 (middle), p. 11 (bottom left); John Cleare/Mountain
Camera: p. 14 (2nd from bottom), p. 15 (top), p. 28 (bottom), p. 31 (bottom left
and right), p. 36 (left), p. 39; Bruce Coleman Limited/Norman Myers: p. 4
(bottom right)/Charlie Ott: p. 12 (bottom)/Chris Bonington: p. 13 (top)/Fritz
Prenzel: p. 16 (left)/John Shaw: p. 16 (top right)/Jen and Des Bartlett: p. 17
(top)/Keith Gunnar: p. 17 (middle)/Jonathan Wright: p. 17 (bottom)/Chris
Bonington: p. 28 (middle)/Eric Crichton: p. 33 (left)/Nicholas Devore: p. 34
(bottom right), p. 37 (middle right); Cumbria Tourist Board: p. 26; De Beers
Consolidated Mines: p. 38 (top right); Forestry Commission: p. 38 (bottom left);
John Frost: p. 29; GeoScience Features: p. 5 (middle), p. 8 (bottom); Susan
Griggs/John Yates: p. 14 (bottom right); Robert Harding Picture Library: p. 10,
p. 19, p. 30 (top), p. 37 (left), p. 46; Alan Hutchison: p. 30 (bottom); Terry
Jennings: p. 9, p. 11 (top, bottom right), p. 16 (2nd from top), p. 21, p. 27 (left
and right), p. 36 (middle, bottom right), p. 37 (top), p. 38 (top left); Tony
Morrison: p. 32 (inset and bottom); Oxford Scientific Films/G.I. Bernard: p. 23;
Rosemarie Pitts: p. 22; Bjorn Ruriksson: p. 18 (top); Spectrum Colour Library:
p. 12 (inset), p. 34 (left), p. 38 (bottom right); Jenny Thomas: p. 35 (right); West
Air Photography: p. 12 (top); ZEFA Picture Library (UK) Ltd: p. 14 (left)

Illustrated by Ann Barrett   Stephen Cocking   Gary Hincks   Ben Manchipp
Ed McLachlan   Barry Rowe   Tim Smith   Tudor Artists   Michael Whittlesea

Illustrations by Gary Hincks p. 5 and p. 8 with permission from British
Geological Survey.

Pebbles by Brenda Hampton, Headington, Oxford.

Contents

Mountains

The main picture shows mountainous country. Mountains are areas of high land. Usually high ground is called a mountain if it rises to more than 300 metres above the land around it. If high ground is less than 300 metres high it is called a hill.

A few mountains stand alone. Fujiyama in Japan and Mount Kenya stand alone. But most mountains are found in long chains called mountain ranges. The Pennines, Alps, Andes and Himalayas are just four examples of mountain ranges.

The highest mountain in the world is Mount Everest. Its top or summit is 8848 metres above the level of the sea.

A mountain range

Fujiyama

Mount Everest

The inside of the Earth

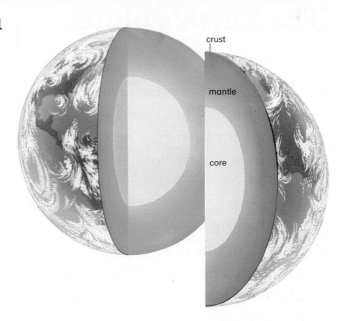

In order to understand how mountains are formed, we need to know what the inside of the Earth is like. The Earth is like a huge ball. It is made up of layers of rock. The outside layer of rock is called the Earth's crust. It is the layer on which we live. The Earth's crust is mostly from 30 to 50 kilometres thick. But in some places beneath the oceans the crust is only 5 to 8 kilometres thick.

Beneath the Earth's crust is a layer called the mantle. The mantle is nearly 3000 kilometres thick. It is made of dense rock. Near the top of the mantle some of the rocks are so hot that they have melted and are a liquid. Because the mantle is being pressed upon by all the rocks around it, the molten rock tries to force its way out. If the molten rock does find a weak spot, it bursts through the Earth's crust. Then a volcano is formed.

The innermost layer of the Earth is called the core. The core is believed to be solid. It is made of the metals iron and nickel.

A volcano erupting

How a volcano is formed

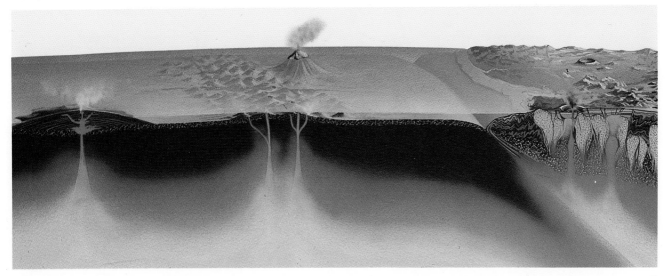

The Earth's plates

On the Earth there are seven huge pieces of land. These pieces of land are called continents. The smallest continent is Australia. The largest is Asia. The continents form part of the Earth's crust.

But the crust does not go all round the Earth in one piece like the skin of an orange. The crust of the Earth is made up of large pieces called plates. The plates fit together like the pieces of a jigsaw puzzle. Some of the plates carry oceans. Some carry continents.

The plates are slowly moving. As the plates move about they push against each other. They cause earthquakes as they move. They push up the rocks to form mountains.

India used to be a long way from Asia. Slowly the plate with India on it moved closer to the plate bearing Asia. The rocks in the sea between India and Asia were gradually pushed up. They formed the Himalayan mountain range. It is possible to find fossil seashells near the tops of the Himalayas.

Some plates are moving further apart. Europe and North America are slowly moving further apart. Each year the Atlantic Ocean is a few centimetres wider.

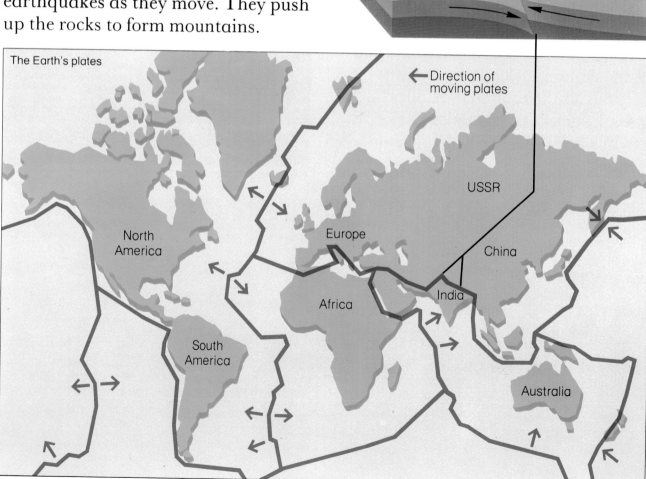

The Earth's plates

← Direction of moving plates

North America

Europe

USSR

China

India

Africa

South America

Australia

6

Block mountains

In places the movements of the Earth's crust bend or fold the rocks. You can see where the layers of rocks have been folded in the picture. Some folds arch upwards forming hills and mountains. Some folds arch downwards forming valleys. Many mountain ranges are the result of folding. The Alps and Pennines are great folds of rock. Occasionally the rocks are folded right over.

As the rocks move they often crack and break. These breaks are called faults. Sometimes great blocks of rocks are pushed up between two faults. These blocks may be so large and high that they form mountains. Some of the highland areas of East Africa are block mountains. So are the Vosges Mountains in France. Many block mountains have flat tops. Flat-topped highlands are called plateaux.

In other places great blocks of rock have slipped downwards between

Folds can arch upwards or downwards

Folds in the rocks

faults. They form what are called rift valleys. A huge rift valley runs through East Africa. It contains several large lakes.

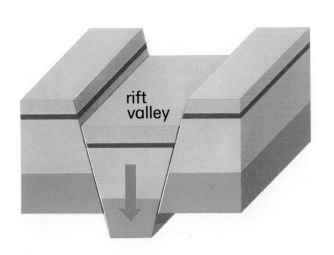

rift valley

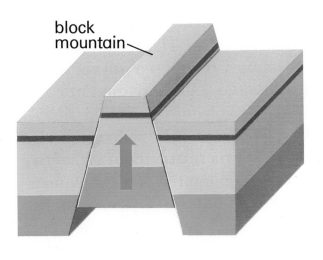

block mountain

Volcanoes

Some mountains were made by volcanoes. Volcanoes occur where the Earth's crust is weak. Volcanoes are made when a crack opens in the Earth's crust. Molten rock from deep inside the Earth's mantle pours out. The molten rock is called lava. The lava cools to form solid rock.

Granite is a rock which was made by volcanoes. Granite has beautiful crystals in it which were formed when liquid lava from a volcano cooled. Granite hills and mountains are found in many parts of the world. Not only lava, but also ashes, steam, and hot gases may come out of a volcano.

When a volcano has erupted many times it may build up a tall cone-shaped mountain. Fujiyama in Japan is a volcanic mountain. So is Mount Egmont in New Zealand. Altogether there are about 450 active volcanoes on land. Not all volcanoes form tall mountains. In some, the lava just seeps out gently from holes or cracks. It then forms thick sheets of rock.

8

Volcanoes do not go on erupting for ever. Some volcanoes may go for many years without erupting. They are said to be dormant or sleeping. Some other volcanoes have finished erupting. They are said to be extinct. Edinburgh Castle in Scotland is built on an extinct volcano. So is Le Puy in France.

Ashes and lava engulfing a house

Mountains are being worn down

How rocks are worn down

Mountains can be worn down by the action of water and ice

Hot days and cold nights

Animals and plants

Even as mountains are being formed, they are being worn away. This gradual wearing away of rocks happens in several ways.

All rocks have tiny cracks in them. When rain falls or dew forms, water gets in these cracks. If it freezes, the water turns to ice. When water turns to ice it expands or gets bigger. The ice presses hard against the sides of each crack. Gradually the rocks weaken and pieces break off.

In hot, dry places such as deserts, hot days and cold nights weaken the rocks. Slowly the rocks break up into smaller pieces. Pieces broken off the mountain slide down the sides. They may form a loose bank of stones called scree.

Scree on a mountain

Rainwater may also rot some rocks. Rainwater is a very weak acid. It gradually dissolves limestone.

All of these things, ice, heat, cold and rainwater which break down rocks, are examples of what is called weathering. In addition, plant roots grow in cracks in rocks. As the roots grow they force open the cracks. Pieces may be broken off the rocks.

9

Rivers and glaciers

Once pieces of rock have reached the bottom of a slope they may be washed away by rivers and streams. After heavy rain, fast-flowing mountain rivers and streams can carry quite large pieces of rock. As the pieces of rock are swept along by the water, they rub and knock each other. They also rub and knock the sides and bottom of the river or stream. Gradually the pieces of rock break into smaller and smaller pieces. And they also wear away the sides and bottom of the river or stream. In this way deep valleys may be formed in the sides of a mountain by rivers or streams. These valleys are often shaped like the letter V.

In some parts of the world there are glaciers. In many ways glaciers are like rivers of ice. Often the glaciers move along river valleys. As a glacier slowly moves along, it wears away the rocks around it. Glaciers make the river valleys deeper and U-shaped.

Thousands of years ago the world was much colder than it is today. The world was in what is called the Ice Age. During the Ice Age there were many glaciers. The glaciers made deep U-shaped valleys. We can still see these U-shaped valleys even where there are no longer any glaciers.

New rocks from old

The mud, sand and stones carried by rivers eventually finish up in the sea. At the same time, rocks by the sea are being broken down into pebbles, shingle, sand and mud. These also pile up on the bottom of the sea. After thousands of years they are pressed into new rock. Limestone, chalk, sandstone and clay were all made at the bottom of the sea. They were formed in layers called strata. You can often see these strata in cliffs and in the sides of quarries.

The rocks formed at the bottom of the sea may be pushed up by the movements of the Earth's plates. Then they will form new mountains. In this way new mountains are formed from old ones. Sometimes the rocks formed under the sea are changed by heat, by chemicals, and by other rocks pressing on them. The rocks formed by volcanoes can also be changed in these ways. All kinds of rocks can be changed. Slate which is sometimes used for roofs was once soft shale. The beautiful rock, marble, which is used for statues, gravestones and fine buildings, was once limestone.

Rivers carry pieces of rock

Rivers deposit mud, sand and stones in layers on the sea bed

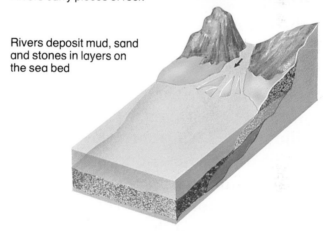
Rock layers, or strata, in a cliff

Fossil shells in limestone

11

Inside mountains

Not all of the rain which falls on mountains runs down the sides in streams or rivers. If the mountain is made of limestone, the rainwater quickly soaks into it. As we have seen, rainwater is a very weak acid. This is because it has dissolved in it some of the carbon dioxide gas from the air. As the rainwater soaks into limestone it makes the cracks in the limestone wider. Over thousands of years, the rainwater may dissolve so much of the limestone that huge caves are formed.

Sometimes a whole stream disappears underground. The stream may dissolve the limestone to form a swallow-hole. Often as water drips through the roof of a cave it leaves behind some of the limestone it has dissolved. This limestone may slowly form beautiful shapes like icicles. These hang from the roof of the cave and grow up from the floor. They are called stalactites and stalagmites. The stalactites and stalagmites may eventually join up to form pillars. Occasionally, the roof of a cave collapses. It then forms a deep gorge. Cheddar Gorge in Britain was once a large cave. But the roof collapsed long ago, leaving the steep cliffs on either side.

The Cheddar Gorge

Stalagmites and stalactites in a cave, and (inset) a swallow-hole

Mountain climates

As you go up a mountain the weather changes. The higher you go the colder it gets. The temperature falls roughly 2°C for each 300 metres you climb. If you climb high enough you will eventually reach the snow-line. Above the snow-line it is so cold that snow covers the ground even on the hottest days of summer.

Mountains are also much windier than valleys and flat ground. The wind sometimes blows across the tops of high mountains at 200 miles an hour. Often, too, the upper parts of mountains are covered in clouds. Clouds are made up of tiny drops of water. The mountains force the clouds to rise. The clouds may rise so high that the tiny drops of water in the clouds join together. The bigger drops of water may fall as rain or snow. Often the rain or snow falls on only one side of the mountain. The other side of the mountain receives much less rain or snow. It is said to be in a 'rain shadow'.

The sun affects the sides of a valley differently. One side may be in

The snow-line on a mountain

A rain shadow
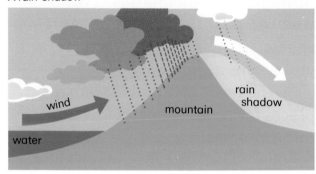

sunshine, the other in shadow. Also, because cold air is heavier than warm air, cold air tends to sink in the valleys. That is why vineyards and orchards are planted on the slopes of a mountain and not in the bottom of a valley. Villages are often built on the slopes of a mountain rather than in the colder valley bottom.

Vineyards and a village on a warm mountain slope
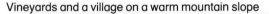

Mountains and people

Many parts of the world are hard to reach because of mountains. High mountains are difficult for people to cross, especially in winter. Places where people can cross mountains are called passes.

Today, some mountains are much easier to cross. Roads and railways have been built across mountain ranges. Tunnels have been made through some mountains. Trains and cars can pass through these. And of course, aeroplanes can fly across mountains quite easily.

In the past, mountains were good places for bandits to hide. Even today some mountain areas are dangerous because of bandits. But mountains also provide peace and quiet. People belonging to some religions have built monasteries in the mountains.

In some hot countries such as India and parts of Africa, people sometimes go to stay in the mountains during the summer. This is because it is cooler there.

Life in the mountains is never easy, though. But some people live in the mountains because they can farm there. Others work in the forests or in the mines. And of course people visit mountains on their holidays.

Entrance to a mountain tunnel in France

A mountain pass in Peru

A monastery in the mountains

Mountain dangers

Mountains can be very beautiful. But they can also be very dangerous. In areas where there is heavy snow, one of the biggest dangers is from avalanches. The problem usually starts when the autumn is mild. Because the ground is warm, the first snow does not stick to it. During the winter the snow piles higher and higher. A sudden loud noise or vibration may make the snow start to slide down the mountainside. An avalanche may bury people or animals. It may even bury villages below. Fences are built and forests are planted to try to stop the avalanches.

Another danger in the mountains is from falls of rock. These may injure people or block roads.

One of the biggest dangers in mountains is the fact that the weather can change suddenly. A fine sunny day may suddenly turn to thick cloud, rain or snow. The low cloud may cause aircraft to crash into the mountains. Many people have died because they were on the mountains when the weather suddenly worsened.

Rescuers searching for an avalanche victim

An avalanche in the Himalayas, and (inset) a road sign warning of falling rocks

Mountain plants

The tree-line on a mountain in Austria

Mountain golden rod

Mosses and lichens growing in a rock crevice

Plants grow in bands or zones up a mountain. As you go higher, the plants of one zone gradually disappear and new ones appear.

On the lower slopes of a mountain there may be forests. These forests are of trees which lose their leaves in winter. They are called deciduous trees. Higher up the mountain there are evergreen trees. They may be pines, firs or other conifers. These trees can withstand the cold and the weight of snow. Still higher it is too cold and windy for trees to grow. The level above which trees cannot survive is called the tree-line. Near

the tree-line the trees may be shaped and bent by the wind.

Above the tree-line there are only shrubs, grasses and small plants. Unlike the trees, these plants can find shelter from the wind and cold. Even so, the plants are small and have deep roots to anchor them. Often they grow very low and form small cushions. They have brightly coloured flowers to attract the few insects which are about at these heights. At higher levels still, only mosses and lichens can survive. These tiny plants can grow where nothing else can.

Mountain wildlife

A condor in the Andes of South America

High in the mountains it is bitterly cold and windy. The ground is steep and rocky. Food is scarce. Only a few animals can live in these high places. They are adapted to life in these difficult conditions.

Animals such as mountain sheep and goats have special hooves. These are hard and sharp and grip the rock almost like pincers. Their hooves help mountain sheep and goats to climb steep rocks without slipping and falling. Sheep, goats and other mountain animals also have thick coats to keep them warm. Sheep and goats eat tough plant materials including lichens, grasses and twigs. Often they climb mountain slopes in the spring and live high up. In the autumn they move down the mountain to spend the winter on the lower, more sheltered, slopes.

Some animals survive the cold mountain winters by hibernating. Marmots and brown and black bears all hibernate.

Mountains are also the homes of eagles, vultures and the condor. These large birds of prey soar above the valleys. They use their keen eyesight to look for food.

A mountain nanny goat and her kid

A black bear in the Rocky Mountains of North America

Undersea mountains

There are many high mountains on dry land. But there are also mountains under the sea. Some of these mountains are as tall as Everest. There are also plains, plateaux and valleys under the sea. In the middle of the Atlantic Ocean, for instance, there is the Mid-Atlantic Ridge. This is a great chain of underwater mountains. They were built from volcanic lava. This poured from a huge crack that opened between two of the many plates which make up the Earth's surface.

Some of these underwater mountains stick up above the sea and form islands. One of these islands is Iceland. The Canary Islands are a chain of volcanoes in the Atlantic. Tristan da Cunha and the Ascension Islands are also volcanoes in the South Atlantic. Many of the islands of the South Pacific Ocean are the tips of volcanoes. They grew bigger and bigger until they appeared above the sea. The Hawaiian Islands are the tips of volcanoes in the Pacific Ocean. There are also several volcanic islands in the Mediterranean Sea.

These islands are the tops of undersea mountains off the coast of Iceland

Mountains and valleys under the sea

18

Mountain myths and legends

Mountains are very high. They are covered with clouds, mist or snow for much of the year. Because of this, people often believed that mountains were the homes of gods and spirits. The people of ancient Greece believed that Mount Olympus was the home of their gods. Certain people in Japan still believe that Fujiyama is sacred.

When a volcano erupted, the people of long ago probably thought the gods were angry. The word volcano comes from the Roman name Volcanus. Volcanus was the Roman god of fire.

Volcanus

Some people still believe that strange creatures live high in the mountains. Some of the people who live in the Himalayas believe that the yeti or abominable snowman lives there. There are said to be two kinds of yeti. One kind is said to feed on people. The other kind eats yaks. The people of the Himalayas believe that the yeti looks like a large ape. No one has ever photographed a yeti. But what might have been its footprints have been photographed. So we do not know for sure whether the yeti really exists.

Yeti's footprints?

Do you remember?

1 What is the difference between a hill and a mountain?

2 What are long chains of mountains called?

3 What is the highest mountain in the world?

4 What is the layer of rock around the outside of the Earth called?

5 Whereabouts in the Earth is the mantle?

6 What is the core of the Earth like?

7 What are the pieces called which make up the crust of the Earth?

8 What causes earthquakes?

9 What are the large cracks and breaks called which are formed when rocks are folded?

10 What are plateaux?

11 What is the liquid rock called which comes out of a volcano?

12 Name a rock which was made by volcanoes.

13 What do we call a volcano which has stopped erupting?

14 What is the name given to the gradual wearing away of rocks?

15 How may water getting into cracks in rocks, make the rocks break up?

16 What is scree?

17 Why does rainwater rot away some rocks?

18 Why do pieces of rock carried away by rivers and streams gradually get smaller?

19 What is a glacier?

20 What shape is the valley made by a glacier?

21 What may happen to the mud, sand and stones which are carried by rivers to the sea?

22 What are strata?

23 How are caves formed in limestone rocks?

24 What are three ways in which mountains can affect the weather?

25 What are the places called where people can cross mountains?

26 What causes avalanches?

27 What is the tree-line?

28 Why do plants growing high up a mountain have long roots?

29 What do mountain sheep and goats have to help them to climb rocks without falling?

30 How were some islands formed?

Things to do

1 Make a collection of rocks

Anyone can do this, not just those who live near mountains.

Look for pebbles and pieces of rock in the garden, at the seaside, by the roadside and in the country. River banks, the beds of streams, road cuttings, old quarries and building sites can also produce rock samples. These last places are *dangerous*, though. Do not go to them without permission, and *always* go with a grown-up.

Wash your rocks and pebbles carefully and dry them. Label each one with the name of the place where you found it and the date. Make a display of your rocks and pebbles for your friends to look at.

When you are searching for rock specimens, always keep a lookout for fossils. Make a collection of these as well. Carefully clean and wash each one. Label it saying where and when you found it.

Use books to try to find out the names of your rocks and fossils.

2 How hard are rocks?

Look at some rocks or pebbles carefully, using a hand lens or magnifying glass. What colour is each one? Is it rough or smooth to the touch? Does it appear to be made of grains? Is the specimen made of crystals?

Is the rock or pebble made up of all the same materials? Will the rock soak up water? Are there any fossils in it?

How hard or soft is each rock or pebble? One of the best ways to test for hardness is to try to scratch your rock with different things. Try your fingernail first. If you cannot scratch the rock with your fingernail, try to scratch it with a copper coin. Next, try to scratch the rock or pebble with the blade of a penknife or screwdriver. If the rock still will not scratch, try a steel file.

If you have one, it is a good idea to fix your rock in the vice on a work-bench. Then you will not scratch or cut yourself when you are trying to discover how hard or soft your rocks are.

Try these tests on man-made rocks such as brick or concrete, as well.

Make a table of your results like the one below. Which is the hardest rock, which is the softest?

Name of rock	Colour	Is it rough or smooth?	Is it made of grains?	Is it made of crystals?	Is it made of all the same materials?	Does it soak up water?	Are there any fossils in it?	Hardness - will the rock scratch with a			
								Fingernail?	Copper Coin?	Penknife or Screwdriver?	Steel file?
Chalk	White	smooth	no	no	yes	yes	no	no	yes	yes	yes

3 Rocks and frost Completely fill a small plastic bottle with water and screw the top on tightly. Put the bottle in the freezing compartment of the refrigerator or in the deep-freeze overnight. What has happened to the bottle the next day? Why is this?

Put a small piece of sandstone, chalk or limestone in a bowl of water overnight. Then place the piece of rock on a tin lid and stand it in the freezing compartment of the refrigerator or in a deep-freeze overnight. See what has happened the next day. Why is this?

Try this experiment with other kinds of rocks and building materials, including small pieces of concrete and brick.

Can you think why, after a really hard winter, the roads and pavements sometimes have large pot-holes in them?

4 Water breaks down rocks You can see how running water in streams and rivers breaks down rocks. Break some chalk into small pieces (blackboard chalk will do). Chalk is a soft rock and will break more easily. It would take a long time for this experiment to work if you used harder rocks.

Half fill a bottle with water. Put some of the pieces of chalk in the water. Put the stopper on the bottle and shake the bottle hard. Be careful not to drop the bottle. Shake the bottle for as long as you can.

Then look at the pieces of chalk. How do they differ from pieces that have not been shaken with water? What can you see at the bottom of the bottle?

You could also try this experiment with small pieces of brick. Do you get the same results?

5 Painted pebbles Pebbles which have been smoothed and polished by a fast-flowing stream or the sea can be made into attractive decorations.

22

Painted pebbles

Wash and dry the pebbles. Then paint them with either water colours or emulsion paint. Once the paint has dried, a coat of clear varnish will seal the colour and give the finished stone a glossy look.

Make paperweights, or simple animals with your pebbles.

6 Layers of rock Find a jar with a wide mouth. Stand the jar in a bowl to protect the table.

Collect samples of mud from different places. Mix several spoonfuls of one of the samples of mud with a cupful of water in an old jug. Then pour all the muddy water into the jar.

Wait until the water in the jar has cleared. This may take several hours, or even a day or so. Then pour in a different sample of mud and water into the jar. Later still, when the water has cleared do this again.

You may have to tip some of the water out of the jar to stop it from overflowing. But try not to stir up the mud at the bottom of the jar.

Can you see why the mud samples form separate layers in the jar? Mud is made up of tiny rock particles. Which rock particles sink faster – the larger or the smaller ones?

Sea-salt crystals

Which of the layers was the first one you put in the jar? Which layer was put in last?

Can you think why some rocks are found in definite layers? If you look at the side of a quarry or cliff, which are the oldest layers? Which layers were made most recently?

7 Grow crystals When the lava from a volcano cools down, often beautiful shapes called crystals are formed.

You can make some crystals of your own if you add salt to some warm water in a clean jam-jar. Stir the salt until it dissolves. Keep adding salt to the water until no more will dissolve. You have now made a strong or concentrated salt solution.

Pour a little of the salt solution into a clean saucer and leave it on a windowsill. When all the water has evaporated, look with a hand lens or magnifying glass at the crystals left in the saucer. What do you notice about them?

If you want to make big crystals,

evaporate your salt solution very slowly.

Make some more crystals in the same way. Try sugar, washing soda, alum, lemonade powder, and Epsom salts. Alum and Epsom salts can be bought quite cheaply from a chemist's shop.

8 Visit your local museum Ask to see their collection of rocks, minerals and fossils. How many of the rocks, minerals and fossils were found locally? How many came from mountainous areas?

You may be able to find out the names of some of your own rocks and fossils if you compare them with those in the museum's collection.

9 Make a book Describe all the things we use rocks for. Collect as many interesting pictures as you can to illustrate your book. Draw some pictures of your own.

23

10 Volcanoes Whereabouts in the world are volcanoes found? Mark the places on a map of the world. Do the marks make a pattern?

Whereabouts in the world do earthquakes happen? Mark these on the map as well. Do the marks showing where earthquakes happen make a pattern? Do earthquakes happen in the same parts of the world as volcanoes?

11 Make a wallchart Collect pictures of mountain scenery. Make a wallchart or scrapbook with your pictures. Write a sentence or two about each of the pictures.

12 Make a model mountain If you have a train set or a model farm, you could make your mountain part of these.

Use a piece of wire netting as the foundation for your mountain. Crumple the wire netting into the shape you want (CAREFUL, the wire may be sharp!).

Cut a newspaper into strips about 2 centimetres wide. Mix a small bowlful of thin cold-water glue or wallpaper paste. Wet strips of the newspaper with the glue or paste. Cover the wire netting with the strips. See that all the wire netting is covered with several layers of newspaper.

Leave your model on one side. When the newspaper has dried out completely, paint your model.

You could if you wished make a tunnel to go through your model mountain.

13 Dissolving chalk or limestone Rainwater will slowly dissolve chalk or limestone. This is because, as it falls,

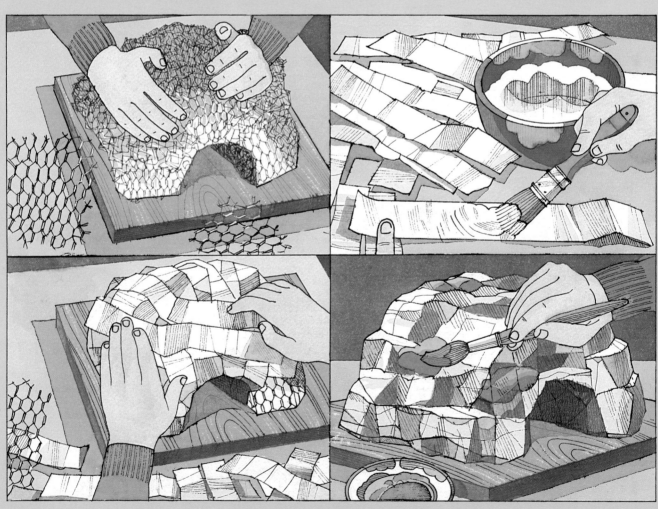

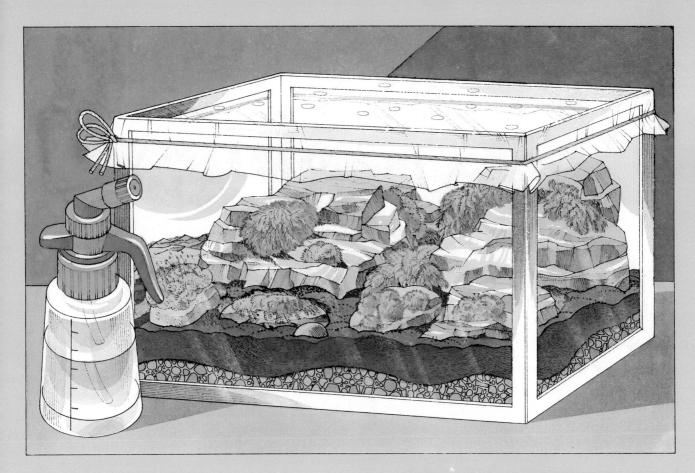

rainwater combines with carbon dioxide gas from the air. This forms a very weak acid which will dissolve the limestone or chalk.

Vinegar is also a weak acid. You can see how chalk or limestones is dissolved if you put a small piece of one of these rocks in a saucer. Do not use blackboard chalk, this is a different substance from the chalk dug out of the ground. Pour a little vinegar on the chalk or limestone. Watch what happens. What do you see? What do you hear?

After an hour or two take the piece of chalk or limestone out of the vinegar. Does it feel different from pieces of the chalk or limestone which have not been put in vinegar?

14 Collect pictures of mountain animals
Stick your pictures in a book and write a sentence or two about each one.

15 Make a moss garden
There are hundreds of different kinds of mosses. They grow in all kinds of places including on walls, in cracks in pavements, on roofs, lawns, the bark of trees, damp soil and, of course, mountains.

Almost any clear, uncoloured glass or plastic container can be turned into a moss garden – sweet jars, fish bowls and aquaria. Choose a container which is big enough to get your hands in.

Line the bottom of the container with clean shingle or small stones. On top of this put a thick layer of moist compost. Plant out some mosses, putting the taller ones towards the back and the shorter ones at the front. Arrange a few stones or pieces of rock amongst the mosses. Spray the mosses with water and then cover the container with cling-film or clear polythene which has air-holes made in it. Do not let the compost dry out and spray the mosses with water from time to time.

16 Draw a graph of mountains

Find out the heights of some mountains. Draw a graph to show their heights. The graph below shows the heights of some of the highest mountains in the British Isles.

What is the highest place near to where you live? Draw this on your graph as well.

Coniston 'Old Man'

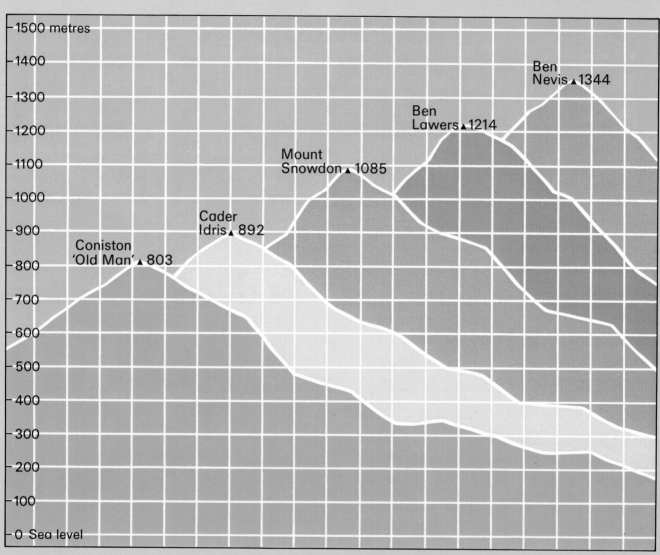

Ben Lawers

Mount Snowdon

Ben Nevis

Cader Idris

Things to find out

1 Look at an atlas. Which do you think is the longest mountain range? Roughly how long is it? What is the greatest width of this mountain range?

2 Some people use the phrase 'rock hard' to describe something which is very hard. Is it correct to use this phrase? Are all rocks hard?

3 Make a list of all the things people use rocks for. How many things can you find?

4 On an earlier page, we saw that rocks are weathered. How does weathering affect buildings, gravestones, monuments and other structures? Is the weathering of buildings worse in towns than in the country? Why is this?

5 Roughly how much would the temperature fall if you climbed from sea-level to the top of Mount Everest (8848 metres high)? If the temperature where you are today fell by that amount, what would it be? What would the weather be like? How would you be feeling?

6 Why is the snow-line higher on some mountains than on others? Find out about mountains which have snow-lines at different heights.

7 Why do roads in mountainous country zig-zag up steep slopes rather than take a shorter, more direct route?

8 In what ways is a tunnel better than a mountain pass? In what ways is a mountain pass better than a tunnel?

9 Lichens are simple plants that grow on mountains. What is unusual about a lichen? Where else do lichens grow? Why are there not many lichens in towns?

10 Use an atlas to find a road or railway which crosses a mountain range. How long is the road or railway? What places does it join? Pretend you travelled across the mountains between these places by car or train. Describe your journey.

The Himalayas

The Himalayas have the highest peaks and deepest valleys on Earth. They stretch across parts of China, India, Tibet and Nepal. The highest mountain in the world, Mount Everest, is in the Himalayas.

The upper parts of the Himalayas are always covered with snow. Neither people nor animals can live on the high peaks. This is because the air is so 'thin'. The higher you go above the Earth, the less air there is. High in the Himalayas there is very little air. Since there is so little air there is not enough oxygen for people to breathe.

However, the lower slopes of the Himalayas have a pleasant climate. The soil is fertile and well-drained. Crops such as tea and potatoes are grown, and there are orchards of apple, apricot and almond trees. Many of the mountain slopes are cut into terraces. Crops like wheat, maize and rice are grown on these terraces.

Terraced fields in the Himalayas

Three Himalayan peaks (left to right): Nuptse, 8,793 m.; Mount Everest, 8,848 m.; and Lhotse, 8,500 m.

Climbing Everest

Mount Everest is 8848 metres high. Until 1953, nobody had ever climbed to the summit of Everest. Then in that year Everest was climbed by Edmund Hillary from New Zealand and Norgay Tenzing from Nepal. There had been eleven previous expeditions to Everest. All of them failed and several climbers had been killed.

Hillary's party set off from Katmandu in Nepal in March 1953. The expedition had 300 porters from Nepal to carry their tents and equipment. On the 28th of May, Hillary and Tenzing left the rest of the party. They were going to try to climb the last part of Everest. The temperature was −28°C, and howling gales were blowing. Hillary and Tenzing made a camp out of solid ice.

The next day the climbers used their ice-picks to hack their way up the mountain. They had to breathe oxygen from bottles on their backs because the air was too thin to breathe. Just below the summit a large lump of rock and ice blocked their way. Eventually Hillary found a crack just wide enough for him and Tenzing to crawl through. They squeezed through and at last they were standing on the summit of Everest. They were higher than people had ever climbed before.

29

The changing Himalayas

The Himalayas are very important to India and Pakistan. These mountains are covered by huge areas of ice and snow. Several large rivers are fed by this ice and snow. The rivers provide water for people and crops in India and Pakistan.

But the Himalayas are changing. In the last 20 or 30 years the population of Nepal has doubled. There is not enough food and firewood to go round. Trees have been cut down to make new fields. The trees have also been used for firewood. Normally the tree roots act like a sponge. They soak up the heavy rain and let it go slowly. The tree roots hold the soil in place.

Now when it rains on the Himalayas, the rivers overflow. Flooding occurs in the valleys and plains below and right across India. The soil on the slopes is washed away. And even the terraces and villages have been washed away. To stop these things happening new trees are being planted. But it will be many years before the damage is repaired.

Floods on the plains of India

Soil erosion in the Himalayas

The Alps

The Alps stretch across parts of France, Switzerland, Italy and Austria. They were originally formed millions of years ago under the sea. During the Ice Age large glaciers carved deep valleys down the slopes of the Alps. Most of these glaciers melted, although a few remain. When the glaciers melted, beautiful lakes were formed in some of the valleys.

Often forests cover the lower slopes of the Alps. Above the forests is grassland. Farmers grow crops in the valleys. There are also orchards and vineyards on the lower slopes.

Cattle are kept for meat and milk. Some of the milk is made into cheese and chocolate. In the winter the cattle are kept in sheds in the valleys. In summer they are taken up to the high grassland to feed.

Some of the farmers live in small houses high in the mountains during the summer. From there they look after the cows. This is called transhumance farming.

Mountain summer homes and summer grazing

31

The Andes

The Andes mountains are in South America. They run all the way down the western side of that continent. The peaks are so high that, even at the Equator, they are covered with snow. After the Himalayas, the Andes are the world's second highest mountains.

The Andes are not a single mountain range. They consist of several ranges of fold mountains separated by high plateaux. People, mostly South American Indians, live on these plateaux. There is not much oxygen in the Andes. The Indians of the Andes have developed extra large lungs. They also have wide nostrils. In these ways their bodies can obtain enough oxygen to breathe.

The South American Indians are farmers. Potatoes and barley are their main crops. But the soil is infertile and the weather cold. And the crops do not grow very well. The most important domestic animals are llamas. These are beasts of burden which also provide milk and wool. A lot of valuable minerals are mined in the Andes. They include tin, copper, gold and silver.

A herd of llamas in Peru

A Peruvian Indian woman

The Great Divide

Australia has no really high mountains. The highest mountain is Kosciusko in the Australian Alps. It is only 2231 metres high.

The longest chain of mountains in Australia is the Great Dividing Range. This is usually called the Great Divide. It consists of several mountain ranges along the eastern side of Australia. The Great Divide affects the climate of a large part of Australia. It stops rain-bearing winds from blowing inland. As a result, the country east of the Great Divide has a wet climate and crops grow well. West of the Great Divide there is an enormous desert.

Many rivers flow down the eastern side of the Great Divide. One of these is the Snowy River. The Snowy River has been dammed. Much of the water now flows west into the desert interior of Australia. This water helps crops to grow where they could not grow before. Large amounts of electricity are also made using the power of the running water. The buildings in which electricity is made using the power of running water are called hydro-electric power stations.

Mount Kosciusko in the Australian Alps

Talbingo Dam in the Great Divide

Irrigation channels fed by water from the Snowy Mountains

The Rockies

The Rocky mountains, or Rockies, stretch along the western side of the North American continent. They are partly in Canada and partly in the United States. For many years the Rockies were a barrier between the west coast and the rest of North America. The early American settlers found the Rockies very difficult and dangerous to cross. Now three railways run across the Rockies.

The Rockies also affect the weather. The western coast of America gets plenty of rain. But the eastern side of the Rockies is in a rain shadow. Much of the land to the east of the Rockies is a hot desert because the clouds have given up their rain as they cross the Rockies.

Several large rivers are fed by the snow and rain on the Rockies. They include the Colorado and Missouri rivers. These rivers are important because they supply water to farmers' crops on both sides of the mountain range. They also supply electricity.

Once very few people lived on the slopes of the Rockies. Now many people work in mines and oilfields which have been built there. Some of the minerals that have been found include gold, silver, lead, copper, iron and coal.

One of the railways that run across the Rockies

The hot desert to the east of the Rockies

The Norwegian Mountains

Fertile farmland at the edge of a fjord

Cows grazing in the summer mountain pastures

The Norwegian mountains slope steeply down to the sea. Between the mountains are deep inlets called fjords. The fjords were formed during the Ice Age. During the Ice Age, Norway was covered by ice and snow. The glaciers carved out deep U-shaped valleys. When all the ice melted at the end of the Ice Age, the sea-level rose. As the sea-level rose the U-shaped valleys were flooded and fjords were formed.

There are so many mountains in Norway that there is little land for farming. Usually, however, rivers flow along the valleys made by the glaciers and into the fjords. Often where the river and fjord meet there is a small area of flat land. This was made from mud and ground-up pieces of rock dropped by the rivers. This flat land is very fertile and grows good crops. It is often the only place to build houses.

As in the Alps, the people in the Norwegian mountains carry out transhumance farming. During the winter the cattle and goats are kept indoors in the valleys. In summer, the high mountain pastures are fresh and green. And the cows and goats are taken up there to graze.

The Highlands of Scotland

The Highlands of Scotland contain the highest mountains in Britain. Ben Nevis the tallest is 1344 metres high.

Ben Nevis, Britain's highest mountain

Most of the Highlands are made up of very old, hard rock. The soil is poor and thin. The rainfall is heavy. Because of these things, farming is difficult. Sheep are kept on much of the Highlands. Wild deer and grouse are also found there, and these are shot for sport and for their meat.

Much of the Highlands was once covered by forests. But most of the trees were cut down long ago. Now a lot of the land is covered by heather. This provides food for the sheep, deer and grouse. When the heather bushes get old, they are burned. Then new, young heather plants grow up in their place.

The remains of heather bushes recently cleared by fire

A grazing Red deer stag

Many hillsides in the Highlands are now being planted with trees. These are conifers such as pine and spruce which are used for timber and paper. Some of the fast-flowing Highland rivers have been dammed. They provide drinking water and hydroelectricity for the towns.

Mountains for sport and leisure

Many people like to visit mountain areas. Some go for the peace and quiet. Others like to walk and enjoy the fresh air and views. Some like to drive along the mountain roads to enjoy the scenery. Still others take part in the more dangerous sport of rock climbing. Equally dangerous and exciting is the sport of pot-holing. Pot-holers explore underground caves and tunnels. Some people also go hang-gliding from mountain slopes and peaks. In the winter, many people visit the mountains to go skiing. Special hotels, ski-lifts and chair-lifts are built for the skiers.

Peace and quiet

Hang-gliding in the Rockies

Skiing in the French Alps

Hiking in the mountains

Many of the mountain areas which attract a lot of visitors are National Parks. The land in a National Park is still farmed. Forests are still planted, and in some places there may even be mines and quarries. But special care is taken to see that the beautiful scenery is not spoilt. The rare plants and animals are protected.

37

The value of mountains

Mountains are made of rock. Many of these rocks are useful to us as building materials. Granite, limestone, marble and slate are used for building. Farmers use powdered limestone to improve the soil. Limestone is also used in cement, paint and toothpaste. Seams of coal are found between the layers of certain rocks. Coal is used as a fuel and also to make many chemicals.

Some useful minerals and metals come from mountain rocks. They include gold, silver, platinum, iron, copper and aluminium. Some precious stones also come from mountain areas. They include diamonds, opals, sapphires and rubies.

Forests are often planted on the lower slopes of mountains. The trees which grow best are conifers like pines, spruce and larches. They provide wood for building, for fuel and to make paper. The slopes of mountains are often used for farming. Sheep, cows and goats can feed and grow on the mountain pastures. Vineyards and tea plantations grow well on many mountain slopes. The rivers in mountain areas flow very fast. The power of their water is sometimes used to help produce electricity.

A granite quarry in Wales

Diamonds from a South African mine

Tree planting in Scotland

Tea picking on the mountain slopes of Sri Lanka

Fragile mountains

Mountains look strong and solid. It often seems as if they will last for ever. But mountains are being worn away. Eventually even the highest mountains will be worn away. As we have seen, ice, heat, cold, rainwater and plant roots help to break down mountain rocks.

Anything which destroys the thin layer of soil or plants on mountains will also help to break the mountains down. If too many sheep, goats and other animals eat the plants, the soil will be washed away. If, as happened in the Himalayas, the trees are cut down, the soil will no longer be protected. When it rains the soil may be washed away.

Even people walking can cause the mountains to wear away. If too many people walk up a mountain path, they may kill the plants. When it rains, water will run down the path. The water may wash away the soil and rocks. A deep gulley may form. Mountains are fragile. They must be treated very carefully.

Compare this picture with the one at the top of page 37. Is this mountain being properly treated?

Do you remember?

1. Name three countries in which you could find the Himalayas.

2. What is meant when we say the air high up on a mountain is 'thin'?

3. What are the terraces for on the slopes of the Himalayas?

4. Who were the first people to climb Mount Everest?

5. Why are the Himalayas important to the people far away in India and Pakistan?

6. What happened when many of the trees on the slopes of the Himalayas were cut down?

7. Name three of the countries in which you could find the Alps.

8. What was left in some of the valleys in the Alps after the glaciers melted?

9. What crops are grown on the lower slopes of the Alps?

10. Where are the cows kept on the Alps in summer?

11. Where are the cows kept on the Alps in winter?

12. Whereabouts are the Andes mountains?

13. What are the people called who live high up on the plateaux in the Andes?

14. How have the bodies of the people who live high in the Andes changed to help them to breathe?

15. Why do the people of the Andes keep llamas?

16. How does the Great Dividing Range affect the climate of a large part of Australia?

17. Why has the Snowy River been dammed?

18. Whereabouts on the North American continent are the Rocky Mountains?

19. Why do a large number of people now live in the Rocky Mountains?

20. What are fjords?

21. How did the fjords in Norway become filled with water?

22. What is transhumance farming?

23. Why is farming difficult in the Highlands of Scotland?

24. Why is the heather in the Highlands of Scotland burned?

25. Name three ways in which people use mountains for sport or leisure.

26. Name three of the rocks we use as building materials.

27. Name three useful minerals or metals we get from rocks.

28. How are the trees which are grown on mountains used?

29. What may happen if animals eat all the plants on a patch of mountainside?

30. How can too many people walking up a mountain path, wear away part of the mountain?

Things to do

1 Build a rockery Rockeries are really miniature imitations of the Alps and the Himalayas. The best rockeries have ledges and grooves in which rock plants, or alpines as they are called, can grow.

Build your rockery in a sunny spot. Natural stone is best but concrete will do. Keep moving the rocks until you get them in the position which looks best. Fill the spaces between the rocks with a good soil or compost.

Easy plants to grow for your rockery are aubretia and candytuft. There are also a number of small bulbs which will grow on rockeries, including grape hyacinths, and snowdrops. It is also possible to buy packets of mixed alpine plant seeds.

2 Pretend you are a mountaineer You are planning an expedition to climb Mount Everest. Write a story about the plans you make, the people and equipment you take with you, and how you set about reaching Mount Everest.

3 Making butter People who live in mountain areas usually make their own butter and cheese from the milk their cows, sheep or goats produce.

Why not try making some butter of your own? Obtain a large clean glass jar.

Choose one which has a screw-top to it.

Carefully pour the creamy layer from the top of a bottle of milk into the jar. If you can, pour the cream from several bottles of milk until your jar is between a half and two-thirds full. Screw the top on the jar tightly.

Shake the jar as hard as you can. You may have to take turns with your friends if your arms start to ache. Keep shaking until a lump of butter forms in the jar.

Separate the butter from the rest of the milk (you can drink this – it is called buttermilk). Try your butter on a slice of bread. What does it taste like?

41

4 Make a model volcano

Make the cone of the volcano with plasticine or plaster of Paris. Do not forget to make a hole in the top of the volcano for the crater.

Take a tuft of cotton wool. Paint it red, orange and black. Stick it in the crater of the volcano. The cotton wool can be the smoke and flames coming from the volcano.

5 The mystery of the new volcano

Pretend that one day you are out for a walk in a lonely part of the country. Suddenly you feel the ground beneath your feet rumbling and shaking. From a crack in a nearby rock you see smoke and sparks drifting upwards. Have you discovered a new volcano?

Write a story about your adventures. Describe what the countryside is like, what you see, how you feel, and what you do.

Can you think of a funny explanation for the ground rumbling and shaking, and for the smoke and sparks coming from the rocks? Include this in your story.

6 Making fossils

You can make some 'fossils' of your own with plaster of Paris.

Begin by putting a layer of plasticine in the bottom of a clean margarine tub. Make the layer of plasticine 1 to 2 centimetres thick. Smooth the surface of the plasticine with a flat piece of wood.

Press some shapes down into the plasticine. You could use a seashell, a thick leaf, a twig, or even objects like a button or a key. Carefully remove the shapes from the plasticine, so that a clear impression of each is left (see illustrations opposite).

Mix up some plaster of Paris in a clean jar. Half fill the jar with water. Add a spoonful of plaster of Paris powder to the water and stir it with a clean stick. Keep adding powder and stirring until the mixture feels like thin custard.

Carefully pour the liquid plaster into the margarine tub. Fill the tub nearly to the top. Leave the plaster for an hour or two or, better still, overnight, until the plaster has set hard. Then break away the plastic tub. Carefully peel off the plasticine. Clean your fossil with a soft brush and paint it with poster paint or emulsion paint.

7 Using a compass

If you walk in the mountains, it is essential to take a compass in case the weather turns bad and you lose your way.

Learn how a compass works. Take a compass into the garden or playground. Set the compass so that the North on the scale and the point of the needle are both pointing in the same direction.

Make lists of the trees, buildings and places which are to the north, south, east and west of where you are standing.

You can make a very simple compass if you have a bar magnet. Cut a strip of cloth about 3 centimetres wide and 15 centimetres long. Make a hole in the centre of each end of the piece of cloth. Take a

short length of string and tie one end into each hole in the cloth. You have now made a sling.

Place the bar magnet in the sling. Hang the sling up by the loop of string away from

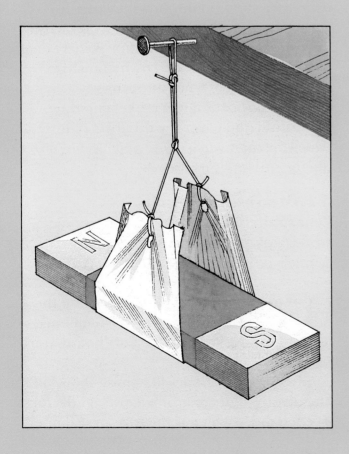

metal objects. Which way does the magnet point? Push the magnet slightly. What happens? Does the magnet always point the same way?

8 Water dissolves substances from rocks Water dissolves some of the substances, called mineral salts, in rocks as it flows over them. This helps to break the rocks down. Plants take up some of these mineral salts through their roots and use them as food.

You can see these mineral salts if you half fill a clean jar with water from a river, stream, lake or pond.

Take a circular filter paper or cut a circle from blotting paper. Fold the paper as shown in the picture.

Moisten the inside of a funnel with water and place the cone of paper inside it. Stand the funnel over another clean jar and slowly and carefully pour your sample of water into the paper. The paper sieves out, or filters, the small pieces of material floating in the water, so that the water now looks perfectly clean.

Put some of this clear water in a clean

jars with hot water. (The spoons will stop the jars from breaking).

Carefully add washing soda to both jars and stir it in. Keep adding washing soda until no more will dissolve. Hang a piece of string from the jars. Put the saucer under the centre of the string.

The washing soda solution will soak along the string. It will drip off the string into the saucer forming a stalactite and stalagmite.

Try this experiment with sugar or salt to see if you get the same results.

10 Make a collage
Use cut-out pictures to make one large interesting picture about mountains and the people, plants and animals who live near them.

11 A mudpie mountain
If you can obtain permission, make a mudpie mountain in the garden. Pat the mud down smooth. Push some stones into the mud and then let it dry.

Water your mountain with water from a watering can. Where does the water wash away, or erode your mountain? Where does the mud which is eroded away finish up? Keep a record of what happens.

What happens if you make a mudpie mountain and cover it with grass plants? Does the mud wash away now? What effect do the grass plants have?

12 Mountain tunnels
Nowadays tunnels are sometimes used to carry roads or railways through mountains. Most tunnels have a curved arch roof. Why is this?

Obtain three pieces of thin card, all the same size. You also need a wooden plank, some thin strips of wood or cardboard, and some drawing pins.

Make tunnel shapes like those shown in the picture. Put coins or weights on the top of each to see which is the strongest shape.

white saucer. Leave the saucer of water near a radiator or on a sunny windowsill. The water will evaporate and you will see the mineral salts left around the saucer. What colour are the mineral salts? Compare different samples of water. Which contains the most mineral salts?

9 Model stalactites and stalagmites
Here is an experiment which shows you the way in which stalagmites and stalactites are formed.

You need two clean jam-jars, some metal spoons, a length of fairly thick string, a saucer, and some washing soda. You also need a tray to stand all these other things in.

Stand a metal spoon in each of the two jars. Ask a grown-up to half fill each of the

13 Collect chocolate wrappers

Collect different kinds of milk chocolate wrappers. Mount them on sheets of card or in a scrapbook. In what countries was the chocolate made? How many of these countries are mountainous?

14 Making rock cakes

Making rock cakes will not teach you much about rocks but these cakes are easy to make and good to eat.

You will need:

225g self-raising flour
125g margarine
125g castor sugar
125g dried fruit
1 egg
about 2 tablespoons of milk
a grown-up to help

What you do:

Sieve the flour into a bowl.

Rub in the margarine until the mixture looks like fine breadcrumbs.

Add the sugar and dried fruit and stir these into the mixture.

Beat the egg and milk together and add these to the flour mixture. Mix everything together with a fork. The mixture should be stiff but not too sticky, and it should leave the sides of the mixing bowl clean.

Spoon out the mixture into 12 equal-sized 'heaps' on a well greased baking tray. Do not make the heaps too smooth on top. You want them to look like rocks when they are cooked.

Bake your rock cakes in a hot oven (220°–230°C, 425–450°F, Gas Mark 6–7) for 12 to 15 minutes. Ask a grown-up to test the cakes for you to see when they are properly cooked.

Cool the rock cakes on a wire tray. They are best eaten the same day.

If you want your rock cakes to look as if they have frost on them, dust the tops with sugar before you bake them.

15 Collect stamps

Make a collection of postage stamps which show pictures of mountains or volcanoes. Display your stamps in an album or on a wall chart. Write a sentence or two about each of the stamps, the mountains or volcanoes they show, and the countries the stamps came from.

Things to find out

1 How do maps show mountains? Look at different maps and atlases to find out. What are the lines called on a map which join places with the same height above sea level?

Copy a mountain range from a map or atlas into your notebook. Try to use the same colours as the map or atlas does.

2 Find out how fossils were formed. In what kinds of rocks are they found? What can we learn from fossils?

3 Choose an animal which lives in the mountains. Find out all you can about it. How is it able to survive in the mountains? Collect as many pictures as you can about your chosen animal. Make a book about your animal.

4 Find out all you can about the life and work of sheep farmers who work in mountain areas. When and where are the lambs born? When are the sheep sheared? What happens to the sheep in winter? Where are the sheep sold?

5 Find out all you can about the kinds of clothes people should wear when walking in the mountains. What kind of shoes should they wear? What else should they do to make certain they are safe?

6 Houses in the Alps have roofs which overhang the walls. Why do you think this is? Try to find out.

7 Climbers on high mountains take bottles of air or oxygen with them so that they can breathe where the air is 'thin'. What other people have to take bottles of air or oxygen with them during their work or hobbies?

8 Find out the names of some large towns in Canada and the United States of America which have been built in the Rocky Mountains. Why were these towns built there?

9 The Khyber Pass is a mountain pass. What mountain range does it cross? What two countries does it link? Why is the Khyber Pass famous?

10 Find out all you can about vineyards. What is grown in a vineyard? How is the crop looked after? How is it used?

11 In 218 BC the Carthaginian general Hannibal led his soldiers, their horses and 38 elephants from Spain, through France and across the Alps into Italy. Hannibal planned to attack the Romans.

Look at a map. Find a route which Hannibal might have taken. What difficulties would Hannibal have met with on his journey?

Draw a picture or write a story about Hannibal and his journey.

12 What mountain areas do people most often visit for holidays? Look at travel agents' advertisements and brochures to find out. What are the attractions of these places to holiday-makers?

13 Find out about the National Parks in the area where you live. Are any of them mountainous? Why were they chosen to be National Parks?

Glossary

Here are the meanings of some words which you might have met for the first time in this book.

Avalanche: a huge mass of snow, mixed with stones and soil, which falls down a mountain into the valley below.

Block mountains: flattish mountains formed where a large block of land has been pushed up between two roughly parallel faults.

Continent: one of the large pieces of land on the Earth's surface.

Core: the centre of the Earth. The core is thought to be solid.

Crust: the Earth's outer layer of rock on which we live.

Deciduous trees: trees which shed their leaves in winter.

Earthquakes: a violent shaking of the ground caused by movement of the Earth's plates.

Erosion: the natural wearing away of the land at the surface of the Earth.

Fault: a large crack or break in a series of rocks. The rocks on one or both sides of the fault may slip up or down.

Fjord: a steep-sided valley worn out by a glacier and flooded by the sea.

Fold: the bending of rocks caused by movements of the Earth's surface.

Glacier: a large river of ice which flows down a valley.

Gorge: a small, narrow steep-sided valley, sometimes formed when the roof of a cave has fallen in.

Hibernate: to sleep for the winter.

Hydro-electric power station: a power station which uses the energy of running water to help make electricity.

Lava: the molten rock that comes out of a volcano.

Mantle: the layer of rock below the Earth's crust and above the core. The mantle is believed to be so hot that some of the rocks have melted and are a liquid.

National Park: a large area of land over which special care is taken to see that the beautiful scenery is not spoilt and where the rare plants and animals are protected.

Pass: a narrow passage through a mountain range.

Plateau: an area of high, level land.

Plates: the sections of the Earth's crust. The slow but steady movements of the plates cause changes in the Earth's surface.

Rain shadow: the sheltered or leeward side of a mountain where there is less rainfall than on the other, windward, side.

Range: a row or line of mountains.

Rift valley: a steep-sided valley formed when a block of land slips down between two roughly parallel faults.

Rock: the solid part of the Earth's crust beneath the soil. Not all rocks are hard: clay is a rock.

Scree: the bank of pieces of rock which collects at the bottom of a steep mountain slope.

Snow-line: An imaginary line on a mountain. Above the line the ground is always covered with snow.

Stalagmites and stalactites: pieces of limestone like large icicles which are found in limestone caves. Stalactites hang down from the roof of the cave, stalagmites grow up from the floor of the cave.

Stratum: one of the layers of rocks which were formed under the sea. If there is more than one layer, the word strata is used.

Summit: the top or highest point of a mountain.

Swallow-hole: a hole in the ground down which a river or stream disappears.

Terraces: flat fields cut into the side of a hill or mountain in a series of steps.

Transhumance: the movement of animals up the mountain pastures to feed in summer and their return to the shelter of the valleys in winter.

Tree-line: the imaginary line on a mountain above which it is too cold or windy for trees to grow.

Volcano: a hole or tear in the Earth's crust from which molten rock (lava) flows.

Weathering: the process by which rocks at the surface of the Earth are broken up by heat, cold, ice and rainwater.

Index